Animals of Africa

MEERKATS

by Tammy Gagne

FOCUS READERS

FOCUS READERS

www.focusreaders.com

Focus Readers is distributed by North Star Editions:
sales@northstareditions.com | 888-417-0195

Produced for Focus Readers by Red Line Editorial.

Photographs ©: l i g h t p o e t/Shutterstock Images, cover, 1; pjmalsbury/iStockphoto, 4–5; Red Line Editorial, 6; Alan_Lagadu/iStockphoto, 8–9; tornado98/iStockphoto, 11; W6/iStockphoto, 12; Shumba138/iStockphoto, 14–15, 29; Topphotoengineer/iStockphoto, 16; Aaron Amat/Shutterstock Images, 18; mylifeiscamp/Shutterstock Images, 20–21; AOosthuizen/iStockphoto, 22; Robin Hoskyns/Science Source, 24; PABimages/iStockphoto, 25 (top); bucky_za/iStockphoto, 25 (bottom right); Kung_Mangkorn/iStockphoto, 25 (bottom left); Mogens Trolle/Shutterstock Images, 26–27

ISBN
978-1-63517-267-6 (hardcover)
978-1-63517-332-1 (paperback)
978-1-63517-462-5 (ebook pdf)
978-1-63517-397-0 (hosted ebook)

Library of Congress Control Number: 2017935117

Printed in the United States of America
Mankato, MN
June, 2017

About the Author

Tammy Gagne has written more than 150 books for adults and children. She resides in northern New England with her husband and son. One of her favorite pastimes is visiting schools to talk to kids about the writing process.

TABLE OF CONTENTS

CHAPTER 1

DESERT DWELLERS

The sun rises on the Kalahari Desert. It is time for the meerkats to start their day. A few spend the morning **grooming**. Others lie in the sun to rest. Later, the meerkats will **forage** for food together.

Meerkats live in the Kalahari Desert in Africa.

Meerkats live in the southern part of Africa.

Meerkats live in Africa. They are found in deserts and grassy plains. Many live in the Kalahari. This is a large, sandy desert. It covers parts of three countries. The desert is hot in the day. It is cool at night. Rain is not common. Deserts are almost always dry.

Meerkats live underground. They dig tunnels. The tunnels are called **burrows**. A burrow can be as deep as 6.5 feet (2.0 m). Each group of meerkats has many burrows. They dig them in different places. The burrows can be connected. This helps meerkats move easily from one place to another.

CHAPTER 2

SMALL AND FURRY

Meerkats are small **mammals**. They are approximately the same size as squirrels. Meerkats stand on their hind legs often. They are approximately 11 inches (28 cm) tall when standing.

Three meerkats stand on their hind legs to get a better view.

Meerkats weigh approximately 2.2 pounds (1.0 kg). Meerkats can be many colors. They are often brown or gold. They can also be orange or silver. They have stripes on their backs.

A meerkat's eyes are lined with dark patches of fur. They have dark, rounded ears. The ears lie flat

FUN FACT

Female meerkats are slightly larger than male meerkats.

A meerkat's fur helps it survive in the wild.

against their heads. Meerkats have long, sharp claws. They use their claws for digging.

A meerkat's tail is often longer than 8 inches (20 cm).

FUN FACT

Meerkats are also called suricates.

Meerkats are part of the mongoose family. Most mongoose species have bushy tails. But meerkats do not. They have long, thin tails. These tails help meerkats balance when they stand up.

CHAPTER 3

MADE FOR THE DESERT

Meerkats have fur that is the same color as the sand. This helps them blend into their environment. It is hard for **predators** to see meerkats because of this. Hawks and jackals have trouble spotting them.

Meerkats can be hard to spot in the desert.

Sand scatters as a meerkat digs a burrow.

Meerkats have dark fur around their eyes. This helps block out the bright sunlight. It helps meerkats see better during the day.

Digging a burrow sends sand flying. Thin **membranes** cover a meerkat's eyes. These membranes block out sand. Meerkats can also close their ears tightly. This helps keep the sand out, too.

FUN FACT

Meerkats have wide pupils. These help them see a large area without turning their heads.

PARTS OF A MEERKAT

A meerkat's fur is well suited for its environment. The desert is hot during the day. But it can

FUN FACT

Meerkats have dark skin. It absorbs sunlight more quickly than lighter colors.

be cold at night. In the night, a meerkat's fur helps keep it warm. Its belly has less fur than the rest of its body. When a meerkat wakes each morning, it stands upright. The animal's exposed belly warms quickly in the sunlight.

CHAPTER 4

LIFE IN THE MOB

Meerkats are **social**. They live in groups called mobs. One mob can include as many as 50 meerkats. Adult females give birth to two to four babies each year. The babies are called pups.

A female meerkat cares for her two pups.

A meerkat mob looks out for predators.

Meerkats work together. Not only mothers care for the pups. Fathers and siblings help raise them. One or two meerkats watch for predators. If they sense danger, they alert the others. The lookouts make a high-pitched call. The rest of the mob then dashes for the nearest burrow. Adults take turns being lookouts. This allows meerkats to spend part of the day foraging.

Meerkats are **carnivores**. A meerkat might eat insects and lizards. They also eat small birds.

FUN FACT

Sometimes the lookouts mistake a passing airplane for a predator.

A meerkat eats a scorpion.

Meerkats even eat scorpions. A scorpion has a harmful stinger. The meerkat must remove the stinger before eating the scorpion.

MEERKAT LIFE CYCLE

A female has two to four pups each year.

Young meerkats are raised by the members of a mob.

Meerkats live approximately eight years in the wild.

THAT'S AMAZING!

MOB DEFENSE

Meerkats protect their territories. When another mob gets too close, meerkats gather together. They stand upright. They puff up their fur to look big and fierce. Sometimes they scare away the strangers. They try to avoid a fight. But sometimes they charge at the approaching enemies. They use their sharp claws and teeth to fight. Meerkats often fight to the death to protect their homes. Large mobs have the best chance of winning these battles. Having good lookouts also gives a mob an advantage in these territory wars.

A mob protects its territory.

FOCUS ON

MEERKATS

Write your answers on a separate piece of paper.

1. Write a sentence that explains the main idea of Chapter 1.
2. What do you think is the meerkat's best trait? Explain your answer.
3. Approximately how many meerkats can be found in a mob?
    - A. 50
    - B. 75
    - C. 40
4. Why might it be hard for meerkats to hide from predators in a climate with snow?
    - A. They are not good at hiding.
    - B. Their tan coats cannot blend in with the white snow.
    - C. They cannot dig into the snow.

5. What does **raise** mean in this book?

Not only mothers care for the pups. Fathers and siblings help ***raise*** *them.*

A. to gather
B. to lift up
C. to care for

6. What does **bushy** mean in this book?

Most mongoose species have ***bushy*** *tails. But meerkats do not. They have long, thin tails.*

A. fluffy
B. spiky
C. smooth

Answer key on page 32.

GLOSSARY

burrows
Large underground tunnel systems used as a home.

carnivores
Animals that eat meat.

forage
To search for food.

grooming
Cleaning and caring for.

mammals
Animals that give birth to live babies, have fur or hair, and produce milk.

membranes
Thin layers of tissue found in animals or plants.

predators
Animals that hunt other animals for food.

pupils
The dark centers of the eyes that allow light to enter.

social
Likely to spend time with other animals of the same type.

TO LEARN MORE

BOOKS

Gregory, Josh. *Meerkats*. New York: Scholastic, 2016.

Sartori, Breanne. *Meerkats: Amazing Pictures and Facts About Meerkats*. CreateSpace Publishing, 2014.

Spilsbury, Louise. *A Mob of Meerkats and Other Mammal Groups*. Chicago: Heinemann Library, 2013.

NOTE TO EDUCATORS

Visit **www.focusreaders.com** to find lesson plans, activities, links, and other resources related to this title.

INDEX

Answer Key: 1. Answers will vary; **2.** Answers will vary; **3.** A; **4.** B; **5.** C; **6.** A